That's My Dog
BULLDOGS

by Marie Pearson

FOCUS
READERS

FOCUS
READERS

www.focusreaders.com

Focus Readers is distributed by North Star Editions:
sales@northstareditions.com | 888-417-0195

Produced for Focus Readers by Red Line Editorial.

Photographs ©: apomares/iStockphoto, cover, 1 , 4–5; John Bazemore/AP Images, 6; Monkey Business Images/iStockphoto, 8–9; *The dog, in health and disease* by John Henry Walsh/Oxford University, 10; *The dog book. A popular history of the dog, with practical information as to care and management of house, kennel, and exhibition dogs; and descriptions of all the important breeds* by James Watson/Cornell University Library, 13; Grigorita Ko/Shutterstock Images, 14–15; Ezzolo/Shutterstock Images, 16–17; WilleeCole/iStockphoto, 19; Twinkle Studio/Shutterstock Images, 20, 29; Runa Kazakova/Shutterstock Images, 22–23; Lise Gagne/iStockphoto, 24; WilleeCole Photography/Shutterstock Images, 26

ISBN
978-1-63517-539-4 (hardcover)
978-1-63517-611-7 (paperback)
978-1-63517-755-8 (ebook pdf)
978-1-63517-683-4 (hosted ebook)

Library of Congress Control Number: 2017948114

Printed in the United States of America
Mankato, MN
November, 2017

About the Author

Marie Pearson is a children's book editor and lifelong dog lover. She once worked as a dog groomer, and today she enjoys competing in a variety of dog sports with her Australian shepherd and standard poodle.

TABLE OF CONTENTS

CHAPTER 1

FAMOUS MASCOTS

Bulldogs are well known for their looks. Their flat and wrinkled faces can appear to smile or frown. Bulldogs are not very **athletic**. But their tough appearance makes them popular **mascots**.

 Bulldogs have many wrinkles.

➤ **Uga sits on the football field at the University of Georgia.**

Yale University in Connecticut has had different bulldogs as mascots since 1889. Each one was named Handsome Dan.

The University of Georgia has a bulldog mascot, too. His name is always Uga. He has his own doghouse on the football field.

Bulldogs are **symbols** of not backing down from a challenge. That is because bulldogs can be **stubborn**. But they are still friendly pets.

FUN FACT

Bulldogs are sometimes known as English bulldogs.

CHAPTER 2

CREATING THE BULLDOG

The bulldog is an old **breed**. The first known writing about bulldogs is from the 1500s. Hundreds of years ago, people used bulldogs to fight bulls. That is how this breed got its name.

The first bulldogs were bred in the British Isles.

▷ Early bulldogs did not look much like the bulldogs of today.

Early bulldogs were taller than modern bulldogs. Their faces were not as flat. Over time, the breed changed to look as it does today.

Bulldogs used in fights had to be tough and brave. They had to be stubborn. The fights were violent and cruel. Many animals were hurt.

Eventually, most countries made these fights illegal. But people kept **breeding** bulldogs. The dogs became friendlier. Even so, they kept their stubbornness.

FUN FACT

US President Warren G. Harding had a bulldog in the 1920s.

At **dog shows**, different dogs are judged based on the standards for their breed. People began to show bulldogs in the 1860s. The American Kennel Club (AKC) **registered** the first bulldogs in 1886. This is a group that keeps official lists of **purebred** dogs.

FUN FACT

In 1880, a bulldog was shown in the United States for the first time. Now many people show their bulldogs.

 The first bulldog shown in the United States was named Donald.

Over time, the bulldog became very popular. In 2016, the bulldog was the AKC's fourth most registered breed.

KITTEN RESCUE

In 2008, Alexandra Breuer was outside with her bulldog, Napoleon. Napoleon normally stayed close by. But on this day, Napoleon took off. He ran to the lake. Bulldogs are not very good swimmers, but Napoleon went into the water. He came back with a bag.

Breuer went to see what Napoleon found. She heard meowing coming from the bag. Napoleon had saved a group of kittens. But they were weak. Breuer helped them get better and took them to an adoption center. Many people came to thank Napoleon for saving the kittens.

A bulldog puppy meets a kitten.

CHAPTER 3

LOVING PETS

Bulldogs have large, short heads. Some have a wrinkle over their noses. Bulldogs' shoulders are set wide apart. These dogs also have short, thick tails. Their tails are either straight or tightly curled.

Even bulldog puppies have lots of wrinkles.

Bulldogs have short fur. They come in many colors and patterns. Some are all white. Others are tan with white spots. Some have coats with a brindle pattern. This can make it look like the dog has black stripes. Most bulldogs weigh 40 to 50 pounds (18 to 23 kg).

FUN FACT

Bulldog ears can have three different shapes. The shapes are known as rose, tulip, and button.

 A bulldog with brindle patterned spots

Bulldogs make loving pets. Some enjoy sitting in their owners' laps. Bulldogs are gentle. But they like to do things their own way.

Bulldogs can get along with kids and other pets.

Bulldogs might listen to their owners only if they know they will get something in return. Treats can quickly convince a bulldog to obey. Owners need to find out what the dog likes. Many bulldogs love getting food as a reward.

CHAPTER 4

CARING FOR BULLDOGS

Bulldogs can seem lazy. They are not very active. But they need exercise to stay healthy. Daily walks will keep them happy. But owners must keep their bulldogs from overheating.

 Three bulldogs go on a walk with their owner.

A bulldog stops for a drink.

On hot days, bulldogs should play inside. Eating ice cubes can help them stay cool, too. Bulldogs also need water to drink. Many enjoy walking in shallow pools to cool down.

A bulldog's wrinkles need special care. Owners should clean the folds often. Wiping with a warm wash cloth will clean the skin. A baby wipe can be used for cleaning, too. However, owners should be sure to dry the wrinkles completely. Removing the extra moisture helps to keep the wrinkles healthy.

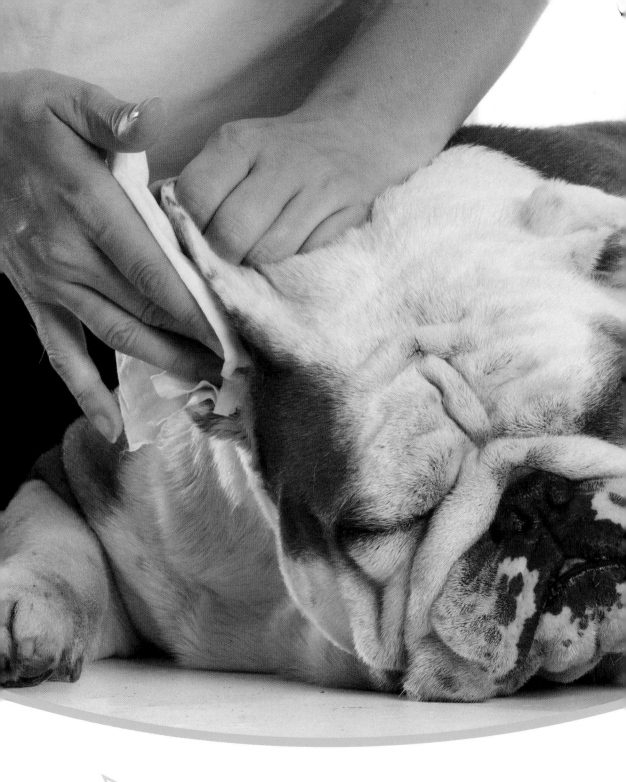

It is important to clean a bulldog's ears.

If a bulldog has a twisted tail, this area needs cleaning, too.

Caring for bulldogs can be a lot of work. But for their owners, the work is worth it. Bulldogs want to spend as much time as they can with their owners. They quickly become loved members of the family.

FUN FACT

A hound glove is a great tool to brush a bulldog's coat. For some dogs, it can feel like a massage.

FOCUS ON
BULLDOGS

Write your answers on a separate piece of paper.

1. Write a sentence that describes the main ideas of Chapter 1.

2. Would you like to own a bulldog? Why or why not?

3. In what year did the AKC first register bulldogs?
   - A. 1886
   - B. 1500
   - C. 2016

4. What might happen if owners do not clean and dry bulldogs' wrinkles?
   - A. The wrinkles will disappear.
   - B. The skin could get infected.
   - C. The wrinkles would get bigger.

5. What does **show** mean in this book?

At dog shows, different dogs are judged based on the standards for their breed. People began to show bulldogs in the 1860s.

    A. take on a walk

    B. take to training classes

    C. take to dog shows

6. What does **obey** mean in this book?

Bulldogs might listen to their owners only if they know they will get something in return. Treats can quickly convince a bulldog to obey.

    A. go to bed

    B. eat food

    C. do what the
       owner asks

Answer key on page 32.

GLOSSARY

athletic
Good at physical activity.

breed
A group of animals that share the same looks and features.

breeding
Causing animals to reproduce.

dog shows
Competitions where different dogs are judged based on the standard for their breed.

mascots
Figures used to represent a sports team.

purebred
An animal born to two parents of the same breed.

registered
Recorded a dog's breed and allowed it to compete in events.

stubborn
Hard to convince to do something.

symbols
Things that represent other things because of a similar trait.